amazing love

joni eareckson tada

ONE EASTER AS I READ THROUGH THE STORY of the crucifixion, I spent several hours deliberating over the words of Christ when he cried in anguish from the cross, "My God, my God, why have you forsaken me?"

The idea that the Father would allow his Son to suffer the torture of crucifixion is beyond me—the humiliation of nakedness, the searing pain, the smell of blood and sweat, the agony of tears, the spit of drunken soldiers, the scorn of a laughing, jeering mob.

When the crowd thinned and the cowards took shelter from the lashing storm, Jesus was left alone. As tears mingled with blood on his battered face, he cried out to his Father—the one who had not once turned away from him in all of eternity. The reply was cold, unmoving silence.

In those horrible moments God himself poured the judgment for our sins upon Jesus. Every sin imaginable: lusting and lying, cheating and coveting, murder and hypocrisy, cruelty and deceit. Of course, Christ had never been guilty of any of those sins. But we are. And every one of your sins and mine was racked up on his account right there on that cross. As the prophet testified:

Surely he has borne our griefs
 and carried our sorrows....
But he was pierced for our transgressions;
 he was crushed for our iniquities;
upon him was the chastisement that brought us peace,
 and with his wounds we are healed.
All we like sheep have gone astray;
 we have turned—every one—to his own way;
and the LORD has laid on him
 the iniquity of us all. (Isaiah 53:4–6)

So where was God's goodness in treating Christ so?

Where was the Father's kindness in turning his back on his only Son while Jesus cried out in horror and grief?

On that terrible, wonderful day, God's goodness and kindness were directed toward you. God forsook his own Son so that he would never have to forsake you! And because of those dark hours two thousand years ago, God can say to you and me, "I will never leave you. I will never forsake you."

As I pondered that amazing thought, I felt ashamed. The goodness of God was indeed leading me to repentance. To think that God's anger for my sins was poured out on Christ—and that he has no anger left for me!

You know what that makes me want to do? Praise him. Thank him. Honor him. Obey him with all my heart and soul and mind.

Unlike Christ, I will never have to agonize over separation from my Father. And neither will you. God poured the full measure of his wrath—the terrors of eternal hell—on his own Son so that you and I could be adopted into his very family. That's how much he loves you. And me.

To read the Bible, learn about Jesus, or find a church in your area, visit **Crossway.org/LearnMore**.

CROSSWAY | GOOD NEWS *Tracts*

www.goodnewstracts.org